Fannie Mae's and Freddie Mac's Financial Status: Frequently Asked Questions

N. Eric Weiss
Specialist in Financial Economics

September 27, 2012

Congressional Research Service
7-5700
www.crs.gov
R42760

CRS Report for Congress
Prepared for Members and Committees of Congress

Summary

Fannie Mae and Freddie Mac are charted by Congress as government-sponsored enterprises (GSEs) to provide liquidity in the mortgage market and promote homeownership for underserved groups and locations. They purchase mortgages, guarantee them, and package them in mortgage-backed securities (MBSs), which they either keep as investments or sell to institutional investors. In addition to the GSEs' guarantees, investors widely believe that MBSs are implicitly guaranteed by the federal government. In 2008, the GSEs financial condition had weakened and there were concerns over their ability to meet their obligations on $1.2 trillion in bonds and $3.7 trillion in MBSs that they had guaranteed. In response to the financial risks, the federal government took control of these GSEs in a process known as conservatorship as a means to stabilize the mortgage credit market.

Congressional interest in Fannie Mae and Freddie Mac has increased in recent years, primarily because the federal government's continuing conservatorship of these GSEs, at a time of uncertainty in the housing, mortgage, and financial markets, has raised doubts about the future of the enterprises and the potential cost to the Treasury of guaranteeing the enterprises' debt. Since more than 60% of households are homeowners, a large number of citizens could be affected by the future of the GSEs. Congress exercises oversight over the Federal Housing Finance Agency (FHFA), which is both regulator and conservator of the GSEs, and is considering legislation to shape the future of the GSEs. Legislation introduced in the 112th Congress, the future of the GSEs, and ways to reduce the cost to the federal government are analyzed in CRS Report R41822, *Proposals to Reform Fannie Mae and Freddie Mac in the 112th Congress*, by N. Eric Weiss.

Estimates of the eventual total cost to the federal government of supporting the GSEs use different baselines and vary widely. FHFA estimates that Treasury is likely to purchase $220 billion-$311 billion of senior preferred stock by the end of 2014. The Congressional Budget Office estimates the budget cost to be more than $300 billion. Standard & Poor's has estimated the cost at $280 billion plus $405 billion to create a replacement system.

Under terms of the federal government's support agreement as amended and effective on August 17, 2012, the enterprises will pay the Treasury all of their quarterly profits (if any). Under the previous agreements, the enterprises paid Treasury dividends of nearly $20 billion annually (10% of the support). Paying the federal government all profits earned in a quarter could prevent the GSEs from accumulating funds to redeem the senior preferred stock. However, it would appear that the GSEs could make quarterly redemptions.

The financial condition of the GSEs appears to be improving. In the first and second quarters of 2012, both Fannie Mae and Freddie Mac reported profits for the first time since the fourth quarter of 2006. Also, the second quarter of 2012 was first time that neither GSE had to request financial support from the Treasury.

Legislation introduced in the 112th Congress, the future of the GSEs, and ways to reduce the cost to the federal government are analyzed in CRS Report R41822, *Proposals to Reform Fannie Mae and Freddie Mac in the 112th Congress*, by N. Eric Weiss.

Contents

Introduction 1
A Brief History of Fannie Mae and Freddie Mac 1
Fannie Mae's and Freddie Mac's Current Status 2
    What Is the Current Financial Condition of Fannie Mae and Freddie Mac? 2
    How Do the GSEs Pay Dividends to Treasury? 6
    What Risks Do Fannie Mae's and Freddie Mac's Financial Problems Create for
        Homeowners and Those Planning to Become Homeowners? 7
    What Risks Do Fannie Mae and Freddie Mac Face in Today's Economic
        Environment? 7
    What Is the Expected Cost to the Federal Government? 8
    What Risks Do Fannie Mae and Freddie Mac Create for the U.S. Government? 10
    Is the Government Investigating Fannie Mae and Freddie Mac? 10
    What Is Happening to Fannie Mae's and Freddie Mac's Affordable Housing
        Initiatives? 11
    Do Fannie Mae and Freddie Mac Have Any Programs to Help Mortgage Borrowers? 12
    Who Manages the GSEs? 12
    What Is Happening to Executive Compensation? 13
    What is the Difference Between the Housing and Economic Recovery Act of 2008
        and the Federal Housing Finance Regulatory Reform Act of 2008? 13
Future 13
    Could the GSEs Return to Stockholder Control? 13
    What Has Conservatorship Done to Stockholders and Other Stakeholders? 14
    What Are Some of Congress's Options for Restructuring the GSEs? 15
    How Can Fannie Mae and Freddie Mac Leave Conservatorship? 16
Context 16
    What Is Conservatorship? 16
    Who Heads FHFA? 17
    Were There Precedents for Placing Fannie Mae and Freddie Mac Under
        Conservatorship? 17
    Why Did FHFA Place Fannie Mae and Freddie Mac Under Conservatorship? 17
    Why Did FHFA Act on September 7, 2008, Instead of Earlier or Later? 18
    What Was Fannie Mae's and Freddie Mac's Financial Position? 18
    Why Did Fannie Mae's and Freddie Mac's Stock Prices Decline in 2008? 19
    What Had Congress Done Previously to Improve the Financial Condition of the
        GSEs? 19
    What Other Actions Has the Federal Government Taken to Address the Financial
        Condition of the GSEs? 20
    Who Has Invested in the Fannie Mae and Freddie Mac? 21
    What Recent Legislation Has Affected the GSEs? 21
Glossary 23

Tables

Table 1. GSE Profitability Since 2006 3

Table 2. Treasury Purchases of GSE Senior Preferred Stock... 5
Table 3. Dividends Paid by GSEs to Treasury 6
Table 4. GSE 2010-2014 Housing Goals and Subgoals.. 11
Table 5. Public Laws Specifically Affecting GSEs... 22

Contacts

Author Contact Information... 23

Introduction

Fannie Mae and Freddie Mac are stockholder-owned, government-sponsored enterprises (GSEs), which purchase existing mortgages, guarantee investors that the mortgages will be paid on time, pool the mortgages into mortgage-backed securities (MBSs), and either keep the MBSs as an investment or sell the MBSs to investors. Congressional charters give the GSEs a special relationship with the federal government, and it is widely believed that the federal government implicitly guarantees their $1.2 trillion in bonds and $3.7 trillion in MBSs. The charters give these GSEs special public policy goals aimed at providing liquidity in the mortgage market and promoting homeownership for underserved groups and locations.

In 2008, the GSEs financial condition had weakened and there were concerns over their ability to meet obligations. On September 7, 2008, the federal government took control of these GSEs from their stockholders and management in a process known as conservatorship. The goal of conservatorship is to restore the GSEs' financial strength and to return control to their stockholders and management.

Congressional interest in Fannie Mae and Freddie Mac has increased in recent years, primarily because the federal government's continuing conservatorship of these GSEs has raised doubts about their future and concerns about the potential cost of supporting them. Congressional interest has been reflected by the introduction of bills to reform or replace the GSEs and by oversight hearings.

This report presents, in analytical question and answer form, the major issues surrounding Fannie Mae's and Freddie Mac's financial conditions, and various public policy options under discussion.

A glossary of terms is included at the end of this report.

A Brief History of Fannie Mae and Freddie Mac

Prior to the development of the secondary mortgage market, mortgage markets were local, and there were significant differences across the nation in mortgage rates and relatively large fluctuations in lending activity. Primary lenders had to balance their lending practices with their deposits received, which led to severe credit shortages during economic downturns, when savings accounts were depleted by withdrawals.[1] This shortage was exacerbated due to the concentration of major money centers in areas like Chicago and New York, far from many who needed home loans. There was no way to move funds from these areas where mortgage money was available to other areas, such as California, where it was in relatively short supply. In effect, this amounted to a geographic barrier that prevented the law of supply and demand from operating on a national level in the home loan market.[2] The secondary mortgage market combined these many regional mortgage markets into a single national market that draws financing from around the world.

---

[1] Michael P. Malloy, *The Regulation of Banking: Cases and Materials on Depository Institutions and Their Regulators*, (Cincinnati: Anderson Publishing Company, 1992), p. 381.

[2] See Carrie Stradley Lavargna, *Government Sponsored Enterprises are "Too Big to Fail:" Balancing Public and Private Interests*, 44 Hastings L.J. 991, 998 (1993).

To encourage improvement in housing standards and conditions and to provide a system of mutual mortgage insurance, Congress passed, and President Franklin D. Roosevelt signed into law, the National Housing Act in 1934.[3] Title III of the National Housing Act established national mortgage associations, giving rise to the creation of Fannie Mae. In its original form, Fannie Mae was a federal government agency that was chartered to support government-backed mortgages and carry out some government subsidy functions. In 1954, Congress re-chartered Fannie Mae as a mixed government and private-sector entity, with a clearly delineated separation between its market-oriented (i.e., secondary mortgage trading) and governmental (i.e., special assistance and managing and liquidating government-held mortgages) functions.[4] In 1968, Congress split the firm into two distinct organizations, with the secondary market arm retaining the Fannie Mae name and the government functions arm taking the name Ginnie Mae, short for the Government National Mortgage Association.[5] The partitioning legislation re-chartered Fannie Mae as a GSE to become completely privately owned with no federal funding. Fannie Mae completed this transition in 1970.

In 1970, Congress enacted the Emergency Home Finance Act,[6] which authorized Fannie Mae to buy conventional mortgages. Fannie Mae bought most of the mortgages from mortgage bankers. Savings and loans, the other major source of mortgage money, were restricted to holding mortgages and were generally unable to work with Fannie Mae. To facilitate secondary market trading of conventional mortgages for savings and loan associations, the act created Freddie Mac as a wholly owned subsidiary of the Federal Home Loan Bank System (FHLBS). In 1989, Congress re-chartered Freddie Mac so that its shares could trade on the New York Stock Exchange, in the same manner as Fannie Mae's.[7] The 1989 act also did away with the separate missions of Fannie Mae and Freddie Mac, with the result that today the two enterprises have similar characteristics.

Fannie Mae and Freddie Mac purchase mortgages that lenders have already made to homeowners. These mortgages must meet Fannie Mae's and Freddie Mac's standards and not exceed the conforming loan limit.[8] These mortgages are guaranteed by the purchasing GSE, pooled into MBSs, and either sold to investors or kept by the GSE as an investment.

Fannie Mae's and Freddie Mac's Current Status

What Is the Current Financial Condition of Fannie Mae and Freddie Mac?

In the second quarter of 2012, Fannie Mae and Freddie Mac both reported profits. **Table 1** summarizes the losses and profits of Fannie Mae and Freddie Mac since 2006. Since 2007, neither GSE has reported a profitable year, but there have been profitable quarters.

---

[3] 48 Stat. 1246.
[4] The National Housing Act of 1954, P.L. 83-560, Title II.
[5] The Housing and Urban Development Act of 1968, P.L. 90-448.
[6] The Emergency Home Finance Act, P.L. 91-351.
[7] The Financial Institutions Reform, Recovery, and Enforcement Act of 1989, P.L. 101-73.
[8] CRS Report RS22172, *The Conforming Loan Limit*, by N. Eric Weiss and Sean M. Hoskins.

Table 1. GSE Profitability Since 2006

($ in millions)

Quarter	Fannie Mae	Freddie Mac
1st Quarter 2006	$2,026	$1,942
2nd Quarter 2006	2,058	1,336
3rd Quarter 2006	-629	-550
4th Quarter 2006	604	401
Full Year 2006	**4,059**	**2,327**
1st Quarter 2007	961	-133
2nd Quarter 2007	1,947	729
3rd Quarter 2007	-1,399	-1,238
4th Quarter 2007	-3,559	-2,452
Full Year 2007	**-2,050**	**-3,094**
1st Quarter 2008	-2,186	-151
2nd Quarter 2008	-2,300	-821
3rd Quarter 2008	-28,994	-25,295
4th Quarter 2008	-25,227	-23,852
Full Year 2008	**-58,707**	**-50,119**
1st Quarter 2009	-23,168	-9,975
2nd Quarter 2009	-14,754	302
3rd Quarter 2009	-18,872	-5,408
4th Quarter 2009	-15,175	-6,472
Full Year 2009	**-71,969**	**-21,553**
1st Quarter 2010	-11,530	-6,688
2nd Quarter 2010	-1,218	-4,713
3rd Quarter 2010	-1,339	-2,511
4th Quarter 2010	73	-113
Full Year 2010	**-14,014**	**-14,025**
1st Quarter 2011	-6,471	676
2nd Quarter 2011	-2,893	-2,139
3rd Quarter 2011	-5,085	-4,422
4th Quarter 2011	-2,406	619
Full Year 2011	**-16,855**	**-5,266**
1st Quarter 2012	2,719	577
2nd Quarter 2012	4,114	3,020

Source: Fannie Mae (http://www.fanniemae.com/portal/about-us/investor-relations/index.html) and Freddie Mac (http://www.freddiemac.com/investors/er).

Notes: Freddie Mac's 2009 annual report revised previously released 2009 quarterly net income. This table reflects the revisions. Amounts shown are "net loss attributable to Fannie Mae," and "net loss attributable to Freddie Mac," which exclude dividends paid to Treasury on the senior preferred stock. All other dividends have been suspended.

The second quarter of 2012 was also the first time that neither GSE had to request financial support from the Treasury (see **Table 2**).

The GSEs' losses that started in late 2006 are notable because, previously, the GSEs had been consistently profitable. Prior to 2006, Fannie Mae had not reported a full-year loss since 1985, and Freddie Mac had never reported a full-year loss since it became stockholder owned.[9]

Two major sources of losses for mortgage lenders,[10] including the GSEs, have been loans to borrowers with less than prime credit (subprime) and certain types of mortgages to borrowers with credit between prime and subprime (Alt-A).[11] At the end of 2011, Fannie Mae held $16.6 billion in private-label MBSs backed by subprime mortgages and held $19.7 billion in private-label MBSs backed by Alt-A mortgages.[12] Freddie Mac held $49.0 billion in private-label MBSs backed by subprime mortgages and $16.8 billion in private-label MBSs backed by Alt-A mortgages.[13] The GSEs have, in addition, increased loan loss reserves in anticipation of continuing losses. If losses on foreclosed mortgages are less than predicted, the reserves could be reduced, which would improve the GSEs' financial condition. If losses are greater on foreclose mortgages, the GSEs' financial condition would worsen.

Starting in 2008, Fannie Mae and Freddie Mac have tightened their lending standards. For example, the average FICO score of a 2007 mortgage purchased by Freddie Mac was 703, in 2008 it was 722, and in 2012 it is 756.[14] Fannie Mae shows a similar increase in FICO scores. Approximately 64% of Fannie Mae's single-family book of business has been purchased in 2008 or more recently; the number for Freddie Mac is approximately 63%.

Since the third quarter of 2008, the Federal Housing Finance Agency (FHFA), as conservator of the GSEs, has asked Treasury for a total of $116.1 billion to increase Fannie Mae's assets to offset its liabilities, and a total of $71.3 billion for Freddie Mac.[15] The second quarter of 2012 was the first time that neither GSE required Treasury's support since the first draw in the third quarter of 2008.

Technically, Treasury support for the GSEs comes through purchases of GSE senior preferred stock. **Table 2** reports the amounts, including the $1 billion of senior preferred stock that each GSE gave Treasury when they were taken into conservatorship. This stock is senior to (has

---

[9] Federal Housing Finance Agency, *Report to Congress: 2011*, pp. 72 and 89, available at http://www.fhfa.gov/webfiles/24009/FHFA_RepToCongr11_6_14.pdf.

[10] Other major factors associated with high losses to mortgage lenders include loans that do not make any monthly repayment of principal, and mortgages with relatively small downpayments to borrowers with weak credit histories. See, for example, Fannie Mae, "Fannie Mae 2012 Second-Quarter Credit Supplement," August 8, 2012, p. 6, available at http://www.fanniemae.com/resources/file/ir/pdf/quarterly-annual-results/2012/q22012_credit_summary.pdf.

[11] Although the names prime and subprime suggest that a mortgage should be in one category or the other, the common industry use of prime, Alt-A, and subprime does not have any overlap in the three mortgage categories.

[12] Ibid., p. 78.

[13] Ibid., p. 95.

[14] Fannie Mae, *2012 Second-Quarter Credit Supplement*, August 8, 2012, p. 8, available at http://www.fanniemae.com/resources/file/ir/pdf/quarterly-annual-results/2012/q22012_credit_summary.pdf, and Freddie Mac, *Second Quarter 2012 Financial Results Supplement*, August 7, 2012, p. 26, available at http://www.freddiemac.com/investors/er/pdf/supplement_2q12.pdf. FICO is a company that provides credit scoring services to lenders.

[15] FHFA, "Data as of August 8, 2012 on Treasury and Federal Reserve Purchase Programs for GSE and Mortgage-Related Securities," available at http://www.fhfa.gov/Default.aspx?Page=70.

priority over) all other common and preferred stock; it is the only stock currently receiving dividends.

Table 2. Treasury Purchases of GSE Senior Preferred Stock
($ in millions)

	Fannie Mae	Freddie Mac
Initial Agreement (No explicit cost)	$1,000	$1,000
3rd Quarter 2008	0	13,800
4th Quarter 2008	15,200	30,800
Year 2008	**16,200**	**45,600**
1st Quarter 2009	19,000	6,100
2nd Quarter 2009	10,700	0
3rd Quarter 2009	15,000	0
4th Quarter 2009	15,300	0
Year 2009	**60,000**	**6,100**
1st Quarter 2010	8,400	10,600
2nd Quarter 2010	1,500	1,800
3rd Quarter 2010	2,500	100
4th Quarter 2010	2,600	500
Year 2010	**15,000**	**13,000**
1st Quarter 2011	8,500	0
2nd Quarter 2011	5,087	1,479
3rd Quarter 2011	7,791	5,992
4th Quarter 2011	4,571	146
Year 2011	**25,949**	**7,617**
1st Quarter 2012	0	19
2nd Quarter 2012	0	0
Total Holdings	**$117,149**	**$72,336**

Source: Fannie Mae (http://www.fanniemae.com/portal/about-us/investor-relations/index.html), Freddie Mac (http://www.freddiemac.com/investors/er/), and FHFA (http://www.fhfa.gov/Default.aspx?Page=70).

Note: Each "total holdings" includes $1 billion in senior preferred stock that the GSEs gave Treasury at the time of their conservatorship agreements. Except for the first draw, Treasury has actually paid the GSEs on the last day of the next quarter: March 31, June 30, September 30, and December 31.

In addition to Treasury's purchases of senior preferred stock, the Federal Reserve (Fed) has purchased GSE bonds and MBSs. In programs that started in September 2008 and ended in March 2010, the Fed and Treasury together purchased $1,135.9 billion in MBSs.[16] On September 21, 2011, the Fed decided to begin reinvesting MBS principal repayments in other MBSs.[17] As of

---

[16] Federal Housing Finance Agency, "Data as of August 8, 2012, on Treasury and Federal Reserve Purchase Programs for GSE and Mortgage-Related Securities," available at http://www.fhfa.gov/Default.aspx?Page=70.

[17] Federal Reserve Bank of New York, "FAQs: Reinvestments of Principal Payments on Agency Securities into Agency MBS," September 26, 2011, available at http://www.newyorkfed.org/markets/ambs/ambs_faq.html.

the end of the second quarter of 2012, the Fed held $855.0 billion of Fannie Mae's and Freddie Mac's MBSs.[18]

How Do the GSEs Pay Dividends to Treasury?

To expedite reducing assets of the GSEs, Treasury, FHFA, and each of the GSEs amended the separate support contracts on August 17, 2012, so that each GSE pays Treasury whatever profits it earns each quarter.[19] If there are no profits, there is no payment. Previously each GSE made quarterly payments on a 10% dividend on the senior preferred stock.

Table 3. Dividends Paid by GSEs to Treasury

($ in billions)

		Fannie Mae			Freddie Mac		
Year	Quarter	Dividends Accrued	Date Paid	Cumulative Dividends	Dividends Accrued	Date Paid	Cumulative Dividends
2008	Q3	$0.01	N/A	$0.00	$0.01	N/A	$0.00
2008	Q4	$0.03	12/31/08	$0.03	$0.17	12/31/08	$0.17
2009	Q1	$0.03	3/31/09	$0.06	$0.37	3/31/09	$0.54
2009	Q2	$0.41	6/30/09	$0.47	$1.15	6/30/09	$1.69
2009	Q3	$0.89	9/30/09	$1.35	$1.29	9/30/09	$2.99
2009	Q4	$1.15	12/31/09	$2.50	$1.29	12/31/09	$4.28
2010	Q1	$1.53	3/31/10	$4.03	$1.29	3/31/10	$5.57
2010	Q2	$1.91	6/30/10	$5.94	$1.29	6/30/10	$6.86
2010	Q3	$2.12	9/30/10	$8.06	$1.56	9/30/10	$8.42
2010	Q4	$2.15	12/31/10	$10.21	$1.60	12/31/10	$10.03
2011	Q1	$2.22	3/31/11	$12.42	$1.61	3/31/11	$11.63
2011	Q2	$2.28	6/30/11	$14.71	$1.62	6/30/11	$13.25
2011	Q3	$2.50	9/30/11	$17.20	$1.62	9/30/11	$14.87
2011	Q4	$2.62	12/30/11	$19.82	$1.66	12/30/11	$16.52
2012	Q1	$2.82	3/30/12	$22.64	$1.81	3/30/12	$18.33
2012	Q2	$2.93	6/29/12	$25.57	$1.81	6/29/12	$20.14

Cumulative Dividends Paid by Both Enterprises $45.71 billion

Source: FHFA, "Data as of August 8, 2012 on Treasury and Federal Reserve Purchase Programs for GSE and Mortgage-Related Securities," available at http://www.fhfa.gov/Default.aspx?Page=70.

Notes: Dividends accrued may not add up to cumulative dividends due to rounding.

---

[18] Federal Reserve Bank of New York, "System Open Market Account Holdings: Securities Holdings as of June 27, 2012," available at http://www.newyorkfed.org/markets/soma/sysopen_accholdings.html.

[19] Department of Treasury, "Treasury Department Announces Further Steps to Expedite Wind Down of Fannie Mae and Freddie Mac," press release, August 17, 2012, available at http://www.treasury.gov/press-center/press-releases/Pages/tg1684.aspx. The press release contains links to the amended agreements.

What Risks Do Fannie Mae's and Freddie Mac's Financial Problems Create for Homeowners and Those Planning to Become Homeowners?

Fannie Mae's and Freddie Mac's financial problems create no risks for homeowners who want to stay in their homes and who do not want to refinance. Homeowners continue to pay their existing mortgages.

Treasury's actions of lending money to the GSEs and the Fed's purchases of the GSEs' MBSs appear to have helped stabilize the secondary mortgage market and provided a continuing flow of funds to purchase new homes and to refinance existing mortgages.

Under conservatorship, the GSEs have become active in loan modifications and the refinancing of existing mortgages that they own. They have raised the credit and documentation standards on the mortgages that they purchase, with stricter underwriting rules and higher fees. These actions are similar to other lenders' behavior during the recent recession and in previous economic slowdowns.

The Economic Stimulus Act of 2008 (ESA) raised the loan limit for FHA guaranteed loans in most high-cost areas of the nation to the same maximum that the GSEs are permitted to purchase.[20] As a result, FHA-guaranteed loans can, in theory, replace most conventional mortgages.

What Risks Do Fannie Mae and Freddie Mac Face in Today's Economic Environment?

In any economic environment, Fannie Mae and Freddie Mac face the variety of risks that many other companies face. The GSEs purchase home mortgages. They package most mortgages into MBSs, selling some and holding others in their investment portfolios. The GSEs finance their portfolios of long-term (typically 30-year) mortgages with short-term borrowing (typically three months to five years). This financing strategy increases the GSEs' profits because short-term borrowing is usually less expensive than longer term loans. At the same time, it creates *interest rate risk*, which is the risk that, if short-term interest rates increase, profitability can be reduced or can even turn to losses. For example, if interest rates were to increase to 6%, mortgages at 5% would not be profitable.[21] To try to reduce interest rate risk, the GSEs use a variety of financial derivatives.[22]

The Federal Reserve has said that it will hold interest rates low "at least through mid-2015"[23] and that it would attempt to lower longer-term interest rates.[24] In the short run, this could aid the

---

[20] The Economic Stimulus Act of 2008, P.L. 110-185, 122 Stat. 613.

[21] Federal Housing Finance Agency, *Report to Congress: 2011*, pp. 30-36 and 46-51, available at http://www.fhfa.gov/webfiles/24009/FHFA_RepToCongr11_6_14.pdf.

[22] A derivative is a financial contract whose value is linked to another financial instrument, price, or variable. For example, two companies could trade a derivative whose value was linked to the difference in the interest rates on 2-year and 10-year Treasury bonds.

[23] Board of Governors of the Federal Reserve System, "Federal Reserve Issues FOMC Statement," press release, September 13, 2012, available at http://www.federalreserve.gov/newsevents/press/monetary/20120913a.htm.

GSEs: they finance mortgages by borrowing for relatively short periods of time and will be able to borrow at lower interest rates. In the longer run, when interest rates increase, the GSEs' profitability may be challenged as they refinance their short-term borrowing at rates that could be greater than what they receive on their mortgages.

In a worst-case scenario, the interest rate on short-term loans to the GSEs could increase enough to cause substantial losses, and investors could stop entering into derivative contracts with the GSEs. This would leave the GSEs, which anticipated being able to roll over their short-term debt, unable to refinance.

The GSEs are also subject to *credit risk*. The GSEs guarantee timely payment of principal and interest of the mortgages in their MBSs. As mortgage foreclosure rates have climbed since 2006, and as home prices have fallen, the value of the mortgages and MBSs that the two firms hold in their portfolio has also fallen. Uncertainty about the duration and severity of the housing slump means that markets cannot now gauge the riskiness of the GSEs with much confidence or precision. The Treasury's support has reduced this risk, but it is not clear if the GSEs will ever return to stockholder control.

Like all other businesses, the GSEs have *operational risk* due to the failure of internal controls. FHFA has directed the GSEs to reduce operational risk by improving their information technology, data quality, and internal controls.

As financial corporations, the GSEs are also subject to *model risk*, or the risk that their models (especially credit models) are not accurate. FHFA has directed the GSEs to update their financial models to reflect changing conditions.

What Is the Expected Cost to the Federal Government?

Estimates of the total cost to the federal government of supporting Fannie Mae and Freddie Mac use different baselines and vary widely.[25] FHFA has estimated that, by the end of 2014, Treasury is likely to have purchased $220 billion-$311 billion of senior preferred stock[26] and the Congressional Budget Office has estimated the budget cost "will exceed $300 billion....but the net effect on federal debt is likely to be smaller."[27]

(...continued)

[24] Board of Governors of the Federal Reserve System, "Current FAQs: What is the Federal Reserve's Maturity Extension Program?" press release, September 21, 2011, available at http://federalreserve.gov/faqs/money_15070.htm.

[25] The Office of Management and Budget (OMB) records only cash transfers between the Treasury and the two GSEs as costs. CBO uses a "fair-value" approach to estimate subsidy costs, which represent "the up-front payment that a private entity in an orderly transaction would require to assume the federal responsibilities for the GSEs' obligations." Another alternative would be to use the cost methods under the Federal Credit Reform Act of 1990, which are used for most federal loan guarantee programs and discounts projected cash flows using interest rates on Treasury obligations. Fair-value estimates use risk-adjusted interest rates.

[26] Federal Housing Finance Agency, "FHFA Updates Projections of Potential Draws for Fannie Mae and Freddie Mac," press release, October 27, 2011, available at http://www.fhfa.gov/webfiles/22737/GSEProjF.pdf.

[27] Congressional Budget Office, *The 2012 Long-Term Budget Outlook*, June 2012, p. 23, available at http://www.cbo.gov/sites/default/files/cbofiles/attachments/LTBO_One-Col_2.pdf and references therein.

Standard & Poor's has estimated that the total cost to resolve (wind down) the GSEs could be $280 billion, and that it would cost another $405 billion to capitalize (create) a new entity or entities to replace Fannie Mae and Freddie Mac.[28]

To keep the GSEs solvent from 2010 through 2012, Treasury has agreed to purchase as much senior preferred stock as necessary.[29] Treasury initially had agreed to purchase a maximum of $100 billion in senior preferred stock from each GSE, and later increased the $100 billion to $200 billion. After 2012, any unused portions of the $200 billion could still be used.[30] Treasury's authority to contract with the enterprises expired December 31, 2009.[31]

Upon entering conservatorship (September 7, 2008), each GSE issued Treasury $1 billion of senior preferred stock and warrants (options) to purchase common stock. If the warrants are exercised, Treasury would own 79.9% of each company. As part of the contracts, each GSE has agreed to restrictions on paying dividends, issuing new stock, and disposing of assets.

The agreements between the GSEs and Treasury set the maximum portfolio size for each GSE at $900 billion as of December 31, 2009, with the goal of reaching $250 billion by decreasing the maximum 10% annually. This 10% reduction applied in 2010 and 2012, but under the third amended agreement between Treasury and the GSEs, the maximum decreases 15% annually until it reaches $250 billion. Under the new, more rapid portfolio reductions, the $250 billion goal will be reached in 2018 instead of 2022. By way of reference, Fannie Mae's retained mortgage portfolio was $789 billion at the end of 2010 and $708 billion at the end of 2011. Freddie Mac's retained portfolio was $697 billion at the end of 2010 and $653 billion at the end of 2011.

The December 24, 2009, announcement said that Treasury would terminate its program to purchase MBSs of GSEs on December 31, 2009. Treasury estimated that the end of 2009 that it held approximately $220 billion in MBSs.[32] Treasury has said that it expects to profit from the spread between the interest rate that it pays to borrow money through bonds and the mortgage payments on the MBSs. Separately, the New York Federal Reserve had its own program to purchase $1.25 trillion of GSE and Ginnie Mae MBSs.[33] The Fed's new QE3 program is purchasing GSE and Ginnie Mae MBSs.[34] The GSEs will guarantee payment of the MBSs.

---

[28] Daniel E. Teclaw and Vandana Sharma, "U.S. Government Cost To Resolve And Relaunch Fannie Mae And Freddie Mac Could Approach $700 Billion," *Standard & Poor's*, November 4, 2010, p. 1, available at http://www2.standardandpoors.com/spf/pdf/events/FITcon11410Article4.pdf.

[29] Department of Treasury, "Treasury Issues Update on Status of Support for Housing Programs," December 24, 2009, available at http://www.treasury.gov/press-center/press-releases/Pages/2009122415345924543.aspx.

[30] More precisely, each the remaining balance of each GSE's $200 billion will be reduced by the positive net worth of the GSE on December 31, 2012.

[31] The American Recovery and Reinvestment Act of 2009, P.L. 111-5, §1117.

[32] Department of Treasury, "Fact Sheet: GSE Mortgage Backed Securities Purchase Program," September 9, 2008, available at http://www.treasury.gov/press-center/press-releases/Documents/mbs_factsheet_090708hp1128.pdf.

[33] Federal Reserve Bank of New York, *FAQs: MBS Purchase Program*, March 24, 2009, available at http://www.newyorkfed.org/markets/mbs_FAQ.HTML.

[34] Federal Reserve Bank of New York, "Statement Regarding Transactions in Agency Mortgage-Backed Securities and Treasury Securities," September 13, 2012, available at http://www.newyorkfed.org/markets/opolicy/operating_policy_120913.html.

Treasury created a Government Sponsored Enterprise Credit Facility (GSECF) to provide liquidity to the GSEs, secured by MBSs pledged as collateral.[35] This facility terminated December 31, 2009.

What Risks Do Fannie Mae and Freddie Mac Create for the U.S. Government?

In the event that it were necessary to dissolve Fannie Mae or Freddie Mac (a process known as receivership), the usual priority of claims on remaining assets is administrative expenses of the receivership, senior and general debt, subordinated debt, and stock.[36] This would seem to place the MBSs with their guarantee at a fairly senior position, followed by GSE bonds, which would be ahead of the government's senior preferred stock, which would be ahead of all other stockholders.

If a GSE were to go into receivership, the value of its MBSs could decline because the value of the guarantee of timely payment of the MBSs would be called into question. If a GSE were unable to perform on the timely payment guarantee, the value of the MBSs would depend on the payment of the underlying mortgages, the rules of receivership, and the government's support for the MBSs.

The eventual value of the bonds would depend on the cause of the receivership and the details of the liquidation process. For example, if mortgage defaults and losses were to increase, the assets available for creditors would decrease.

In the event of receivership, it would appear unlikely that the senior preferred stock would have much value.

Is the Government Investigating Fannie Mae and Freddie Mac?

The existence of an investigation is not usually announced or acknowledged, but there have been media reports that the Securities and Exchange Commission (SEC) is investigating several current or former GSE executives.[37] SEC is reported to have sent formal notice of its intent to recommend civil charges against former Fannie Mae chief executive officer (CEO) Daniel H. Mudd, former Freddie Mac CEO Richard F. Syron, former Freddie Mac chief financial officer Anthony S. Piszel, and Freddie Mac executive vice president Donald J. Bisenius. These notices (known as Wells notices) provide the opportunity to respond to the charges and to persuade the SEC not to proceed with the recommendation to the commission to file civil charges.

---

[35] Department of Treasury, "Fact Sheet: Government Sponsored Enterprise Credit Facility," September 7, 2008, available at http://www.treasury.gov/press-center/press-releases/Documents/gsecf_factsheet_090708.pdf.

[36] CRS Report RL34657, *Financial Institution Insolvency: Federal Authority over Fannie Mae, Freddie Mac, and Depository Institutions*, by David H. Carpenter and M. Maureen Murphy, contains more information on this subject.

[37] Ben Protess and Azam Ahmed, "Ex-Chief of Freddie May Face Civil Action," *The New York Times*, March 16, 2011, p. B1.

What Is Happening to Fannie Mae's and Freddie Mac's Affordable Housing Initiatives?

The Housing and Economic Recovery Act of 2008 (HERA; P.L. 110-289) gives the FHFA authority to set housing goals for Fannie Mae and Freddie Mac. **Table 4** summarizes the 2010 to 2014 housing goals and subgoals. Fannie Mae and Freddie Mac can also meet a housing goal or subgoal by purchasing sufficient qualifying mortgages to mirror or exceed the market.[38]

Table 4. GSE 2010-2014 Housing Goals and Subgoals

Category	2010-2011 Actual Goal	2012-1014 Proposed Goal
Low-Income Families Housing Goal (Fannie Mae, Freddie Mac)	27% purchase money (mortgages used to purchase a home)	20% purchase money
Very Low-Income Families Housing Goal (Fannie Mae, Freddie Mac)	8% purchase money	7% purchase money
Low-Income Areas Housing Goal (Fannie Mae, Freddie Mac)	13% purchase money	11% purchase money
Refinancing Housing Goal (Fannie Mae, Freddie Mac)	21% refinance	21% refinance
Multifamily Low-Income Housing Goal (Fannie Mae)	177,750 dwelling units	2012: 251,000 dwelling units 2013: 245,000 dwelling units 2014: 223,000 dwelling units
Multifamily Low-Income Housing Goal (Freddie Mac)	161,250 dwelling units	2012: 191,000 dwelling units 2013: 203,000 dwelling units 2014: 181,000 dwelling units
Multifamily Very Low-Income Housing Subgoal (Fannie Mae)	42,750 dwelling units	2012: 60,000 dwelling units 2013: 59,000 dwelling units 2014: 53,000 dwelling units
Multifamily Very Low-Income Housing Subgoal (Freddie Mac)	21,000 dwelling units	2012: 32,000 dwelling units 2013: 31,000 dwelling units 2014: 27,000 dwelling units

Sources: Federal Housing Finance Agency, "2010–2011 Enterprise Housing Goals; Enterprise Book-entry Procedures," 75 *Federal Register* 55892-55939, September 14, 2010; Federal Housing Finance Agency, "2012-2014 Enterprise Housing Goals," 77 *Federal Register*, , 34263-34281, June 11, 2012.

Note: Alternatively, Fannie Mae and Freddie Mac can meet their housing goals by purchasing mortgages to equal or exceed the market percentage.

---

[38] Of course, Fannie Mae or Freddie Mac's success in meeting or exceeding the mortgage market's percentages in the various goals can only be known after the year is over. This does, however, provide a way to meet the goal requirements if changes in the mortgage market make meeting the goals in **Table 3** very difficult or impossible.

Do Fannie Mae and Freddie Mac Have Any Programs to Help Mortgage Borrowers?

Fannie Mae[39] and Freddie Mac[40] each have special programs for mortgage borrowers, but only for borrowers whose loans each holds. These programs include allowing certain borrowers who owe more than their homes are currently worth to refinance their mortgages or enter into repayment plans, forbearance plans, mortgage modifications, and deed-for-lease[41] plans. There are also programs to avoid foreclosure through short sales and deeds-in-lieu of foreclosure.[42]

Fannie Mae and Freddie Mac have programs to allow a homeowner facing foreclosure to surrender the deed in lieu of foreclosure and then to lease the home back. The Fannie Mae lease is for 12 months and can be renewed, whereas the Freddie Mac lease is month-to-month. Both programs charge a market rate for the lease.

Information on additional government programs is available at http://www.makinghomeaffordable.gov/.

For additional information on programs to help mortgage borrowers, see CRS Report R42480, *Reduce, Refinance, and Rent? The Economic Incentives, Risks, and Ramifications of Housing Market Policy Options*, by Sean M. Hoskins.

Who Manages the GSEs?

Fannie Mae and Freddie Mac have separate management teams headed by a chief executive officer and overseen by their conservator and regulator, the Federal Housing Finance Agency. Fannie Mae CEO Daniel H. Mudd and Freddie Mac CEO Richard F. Syron resigned when their companies were placed in conservatorship on September 7, 2008. FHFA appointed Herbert M. Allison Jr. as Fannie Mae's CEO and David Moffett as Freddie Mac's CEO.

Effective March 13, 2009, Moffett resigned from Freddie Mac to return to the private sector. He has since returned as a consultant. On April 20, 2009, Allison resigned from Fannie Mae to accept the nomination to be assistant treasury secretary for financial stability (who oversees Treasury's Troubled Asset Relief Program) and counselor to the Secretary.

---

[39] Fannie Mae, "Avoiding Foreclosure," available at http://www.fanniemae.com/portal/helping-homeowners-communities/foreclosure-help.html.

[40] Freddie Mac, "Alternatives to Foreclosure," available at http://www.freddiemac.com/avoidforeclosure/alternatives_to_foreclosure.html.

[41] In a deed-for-lease plan, the delinquent homeowner surrenders the deed to the lender and leases (rents) the home for an agreed-upon time period.

[42] In a short sale, the lender agrees to cancel a mortgage in return for the proceeds from the sale of a home, even though the proceeds are less than the amount owed. A deed in lieu is when the home owner turns the property over to the lender and is released from the mortgage obligations. In both cases, the lender owns the house, the homeowner moves, and the mortgage is cancelled.

On May 10, 2012, Freddie Mac's Board of Directors (with FHFA approval) appointed Donald H. Layton as CEO effective May 21.[43] On June 5, 2012, Fannie Mae's Board of Directors (with FHFA approval) appointed Timothy J. Mayopoulos as CEO effective June 18.[44]

What Is Happening to Executive Compensation?

The Housing and Economic Recovery Act (HERA; P.L. 110-289) strengthened FHFA's regulation over executive compensation and so-called golden parachutes. The senior preferred stock agreement signed by each GSE with FHFA requires the GSEs to get approval for new compensation agreements with executives. The current CEOs each are receiving base salaries of $500,000,[45] but some executives are receiving compensation at higher rates established under previous FHFA-approved agreements.

What is the Difference Between the Housing and Economic Recovery Act of 2008 and the Federal Housing Finance Regulatory Reform Act of 2008?

The Housing and Economic Recovery Act of 2008 is the popular title of the entire law, P.L. 110-289. The Federal Housing Finance Regulatory Reform Act of 2008 is the popular title for Division A of P.L. 110-289.

Future

Could the GSEs Return to Stockholder Control?

In principle, Congress might decide that the changes that FHFA is making to each of the GSEs reduce the risk of future financial problems to an acceptable level and that the GSEs could return to stockholder control.[46]

The federal government's financial support extended to the GSEs could, however, make a return to the prior status problematic. The elimination of dividends greatly reduced the value of the GSEs' preferred stock. Because the appeal of preferred stock is centered on the security of its dividend payments, the long-run value of the GSEs' preferred stock has been reduced. The value of common stock has been reduced because of the termination of their dividends and increased uncertainty over the future long-run viability of the enterprises. Even if the GSEs were to return

---

[43] Federal Home Loan Mortgage Corporation, "Form 8-K," May 10, 2012, available at http://www.sec.gov/Archives/edgar/data/1026214/000102621412000051/f71884e8vk.htm.

[44] Federal National Mortgage Association, "Form 8-K," June 5, 2012, available at http://www.sec.gov/Archives/edgar/data/310522/000129993312001410/htm_45294.htm.

[45] FHFA, "FHFA Announces New Conservatorship Scorecard for Fannie Mae and Freddie Mac; Reduces Executive Compensation," press release, March 9, 2012, available at http://www.fhfa.gov/webfiles/23438/ExecComp3912F.pdf.

[46] For details on changes at Fannie Mae and Freddie Mac see Federal Housing Finance Agency, *Report to Congress: 2011*, pp. 21-52, available at http://www.fhfa.gov/webfiles/24009/FHFA_RepToCongr11_6_14.pdf.

to stockholder control, it is not clear how much appeal their common and preferred stock would have for investors. If the GSEs were unable to raise capital, they would be unable to continue.

The treatment of bondholders could make lending to the GSEs more attractive. While common and preferred stockholders suffered during conservatorship (but no more than they would have suffered from dissolution of the GSEs), payments to bond and MBS holders have continued as contracted. The government's actions could convince bondholders that the risk of holding bonds is less than previously thought. This would allow the GSEs to borrow money by selling bonds at rates very close to Treasury rates.

As the housing market fully recovers, the GSEs could be in a very strong position to purchase mortgages and to create MBSs. For stockholders, the economics of the GSEs' mortgage business could be attractive, but the psychology of the decline in stock prices and the federal government's claim on all profits could potentially offset this plus.

One open question in the GSEs' return to stockholder ownership is the government's decision on what to do with the warrants for nearly 80% of the GSEs' ownership. The government could auction the warrants off to the highest bidder, or the government could exercise the warrants to obtain control of the GSEs as each one's majority stockholder.

What Has Conservatorship Done to Stockholders and Other Stakeholders?

The powers of common stockholders, who formerly elected the boards of directors and approved certain enterprise actions, are suspended. FHFA as the conservator has assumed all of their authority. Previously, the common stockholders owned 100% of the GSEs. As a result of the warrants issued to the Treasury, they could own only 20% of the enterprises. In the long run, 20% of a healthy enterprise could be worth more than 100% of GSEs whose liabilities exceed their assets. In the short run, the price of the GSEs' common stock has declined, but if the GSEs recover, stockholders would arguably be better off compared to their situation at the time that conservatorship was undertaken.

To the extent that current and former employees have invested in common stock, in the short run they have seen a decline in the value of their financial assets; the long-run outcome is not clear. Both GSEs had employee stock and option plans. The GSEs' agreements with Treasury prohibit issuing new stock. Consequently, those programs cannot continue until the GSEs emerge from conservatorship.

GSE employees have been urged by FHFA to continue working as before. While the conservator is authorized by federal law to cancel certain contracts, FHFA has said that current contracts continue to be in force.

To keep Fannie Mae and Freddie Mac solvent (assets greater than liabilities), Treasury has purchased special senior preferred stock. The cash paid for the preferred stock is an accounting asset, and the special senior preferred stock increases the Treasury's equity in the GSEs. This senior preferred stock originally paid annual dividends of 10%, which would increase to 12% annually if a GSE fails to pay the dividend; these are the only dividends that the GSEs are allowed to pay.

On August 17, 2012, Treasury signed new agreements with Fannie Mae and Freddie Mac changing the quarterly dividend to be all the profits earned in the quarter. If no profits are earned, no dividend is paid. Treasury said that the purpose of the change was to wind down the GSEs and to benefit taxpayers.[47]

What Are Some of Congress's Options for Restructuring the GSEs?

Going forward, Congress has many options for reorganizing Fannie Mae and Freddie Mac. It could, also, decide to wind down the GSEs and leave the housing market to the private sector. If Congress were to decide to keep and to reorganize Fannie Mae and Freddie Mac, options include (but are not limited to) the following:

- Congress could make Fannie Mae and Freddie Mac part of the government. Both GSEs were originally government corporations, and this would be a return to that environment.

- Fannie Mae and Freddie Mac could become Federal Home Loan Banks. The 12 regional banks are a collective GSE that is owned by their member institutions, and their stock is not publicly traded. Fannie Mae's and Freddie Mac's stock could become an asset of the Federal Home Loan Bank System or of the individual banks.

- Fannie Mae and Freddie Mac could be split up into a large number of GSEs. Instead of two GSEs that are "too big to fail," there would be 10 or some other number of smaller GSEs that would arguably each be small enough to fail. The GSEs could be split in such a way that they would not be clones of each other and one or two could fail without the others going under. Congress might wish to explicitly state what the risks to stockholders, bondholders, and business partners would be. The competition could mean more benefits from GSE status go to homebuyers instead of the GSEs.

- Fannie Mae and Freddie Mac (and possibly additional new GSEs) could be converted into "utilities." These corporations would not necessarily be GSEs. Each could issue MBSs, possibly guaranteed by the federal government, which would charge a fee for the guarantee. There are a number of options for how the fees could be set. The government could establish a standard fee, or it could auction off the right to issue a specific amount of MBSs. They could sell these MBSs or possibly retain them.

- The government could sell additional new GSE charters to the highest bidders.

- Then-Treasury Secretary Henry M. Paulson Jr. proposed using bonds backed not only by the issuing corporation's legal obligation of repayment, but also by the pledge of specific collateral, as a way to allow banks to supplement or even replace the GSEs' role in mortgage markets.[48]

---

[47] Department of Treasury, "Treasury Department Announces Further Steps to Expedite Wind Down of Fannie Mae and Freddie Mac," press release, August 12, 2012, available at http://www.treasury.gov/press-center/press-releases/Pages/tg1684.aspx.

[48] Henry M. Paulson Jr., Secretary of the Treasury, "Remarks by Secretary Henry M. Paulson Jr. on Recommendations from the President's Working Group on Financial Markets," press release, March 13, 2008, available at (continued...)

For additional information, see CRS Report R40800, *GSEs and the Government's Role in Housing Finance: Issues for the 112th Congress*, by N. Eric Weiss and CRS Report R41822, *Proposals to Reform Fannie Mae and Freddie Mac in the 112th Congress*, by N. Eric Weiss.

How Can Fannie Mae and Freddie Mac Leave Conservatorship?

There are two ways that Fannie Mae and Freddie Mac could exit their conservatorships. If they become financially viable, they could return to stockholder control. If they are unable to become financially viable, they could enter receivership. There is no legal reason that one GSE could not go into receivership and the other GSE return to stockholder control, although this might present some policy questions about the desirability of having a monopoly GSE.

There are several obstacles to a return to financial viability. In conservatorship, the GSEs are balancing their goals of support for home mortgage markets and their goal of profitability. At times, these goals may conflict. The concern of the federal government and FHFA for mortgage market stability and liquidity may take precedence over the return to profitability.[49]

Paying the federal government all profits earned in a quarter might prevent the GSEs from accumulating funds to redeem the senior preferred stock. However, if this payment applies only at the *end* of a quarter, it would appear that the GSEs could redeem some senior preferred stock using funds available *before* the end of each quarter. This would be a way for the GSEs could return to stockholder control, although it would likely take many years. FHFA could prevent (or authorize) this redemption of senior preferred stock.

Context

What Is Conservatorship?

Conservatorship of Fannie Mae and Freddie Mac involves FHFA taking control of the GSEs. As conservator, the powers of the board of directors, officers, and shareholders are transferred to FHFA. A conservator can also cancel certain contracts. Conservatorship is authorized by the Housing and Economic Recovery Act of 2008 (HERA).[50] The goal of conservatorship is to preserve each of the GSE's assets and to return it to sound financial condition that would allow the conservatorship to be ended.

(...continued)
http://www.treasury.gov/press-center/press-releases/Pages/hp872.aspx. For more information about covered bonds, see CRS Report R41322, *Covered Bonds: Issues in the 112th Congress*, by Edward V. Murphy.

[49] Freddie Mac, *Form 10-K for the Fiscal Year Ending December 31*, p. 19, available at http://www.freddiemac.com/investors/er/pdf/10k_031109.pdf, and Fannie Mae, *Form 10-K for the Fiscal Year Ending December 31, 2008*, p. 9, available at http://www.fanniemae.com/ir/pdf/earnings/2008/form10k_022609.pdf.

[50] The Housing and Economic Recovery Act of 2008, P.L. 110-289, 122 Stat. 2654 et seq.

Who Heads FHFA?

On August 6, 2009, FHFA Director James B. Lockhart announced that he would resign in the near future. President Obama named Senior Deputy Director for Housing Mission and Goals Edward J. DeMarco as acting director. On November 12, 2010, President Obama nominated Joseph A. Smith, North Carolina commissioner of banks, to be the FHFA director,[51] but the full Senate did not vote on his confirmation. The President has not made another nomination for the position.

Were There Precedents for Placing Fannie Mae and Freddie Mac Under Conservatorship?

This is the first time that a GSE has been placed under conservatorship. It appears to also be the first time that the federal government has made a continuing commitment to a company (other than government corporations). On a more general level, the federal government has intervened in the past to assist many companies.[52] Since placing Fannie Mae and Freddie Mac under conservatorship, the federal government has intervened to support numerous companies, including General Motors, Chrysler, AIG, and various banks.[53]

Why Did FHFA Place Fannie Mae and Freddie Mac Under Conservatorship?

As regulator of Fannie Mae and Freddie Mac, FHFA announced that it had placed Fannie Mae and Freddie Mac under conservatorship because of their deteriorating financial positions and the "critical importance" that each company has to the continued functioning of the residential financial markets.[54]

FHFA has said that continuing audits of the GSEs determined that their financial positions were weaker than previously thought and that the GSEs were unlikely to survive without conservatorship. FHFA cited previous public statements that the GSEs needed to increase their capital and needed to strengthen management controls over operations.

---

[51] The White House, Office of the Press Secretary, "President Obama Announces More Key Administration Posts," press release, November 12, 2010, available at http://www.whitehouse.gov/the-press-office/2010/11/12/president-obama-announces-more-key-administration-posts.

[52] CRS Report RL34423, *Government Interventions in Financial Markets: Economic and Historic Analysis of Subprime Mortgage Options*, by N. Eric Weiss, discusses some of these actions.

[53] CRS Report RS22956, *The Cost of Government Financial Interventions, Past and Present*, by Baird Webel, Marc Labonte, and N. Eric Weiss; also CRS Report R41427, *Troubled Asset Relief Program (TARP): Implementation and Status*, by Baird Webel.

[54] FHFA, "Statement of FHFA Director James B. Lockhart," September 7, 2008, available at http://www.fhfa.gov/webfiles/23/FHFAStatement9708final.pdf. See, also, Henry M. Paulson Jr., *On the Brink: Inside the Race to Stop the Collapse of the Global Financial System* (New York: Business Plus, 2010).

Why Did FHFA Act on September 7, 2008, Instead of Earlier or Later?

FHFA, in general, followed the same approach that the Federal Deposit Insurance Corporation (FDIC) uses when it places a bank in conservatorship: a series of requests for changes to the corporation and to increase capital followed by a sudden takeover. Providing a deadline could provide the regulated entity with an incentive to take risky gambles in a last attempt to avoid being seized by the government. The FDIC usually seizes a bank by suddenly showing up on a Friday afternoon, closing the bank, and locking the doors. This gives the FDIC time to make necessary changes over the weekend and resume business operations on the next business day.

According to media reports at the time, some large foreign investors had been reducing their holdings of GSE debt, MBSs, and stock.[55] This would have made it more difficult for the GSEs to borrow money to finance their portfolios going forward. For example, Bank of China Ltd. is reported to have sold or not replaced $4.6 billion of maturing GSE debt, which reduced its GSE debt holdings to $17.3 billion as of June 30, 2008. These same media reported that Treasury officials contacted foreign central banks and others to reassure them of the creditworthiness of GSE debt.

What Was Fannie Mae's and Freddie Mac's Financial Position?

In placing the GSEs under conservatorship, their new regulator, FHFA, said that they needed assistance to survive. FHFA reported that changes in the economy and the GSEs' slow recovery from their earlier accounting and financial problems reduced their financial strength.[56]

The Office of Federal Housing Enterprise Oversight (OFHEO), which had been Fannie Mae's and Freddie Mac's safety and soundness regulator before July 30, 2008, repeatedly said that the GSEs had adequate capital.[57] In other words, according to OFHEO, the GSEs had sufficient funds to survive their financial difficulties. Because details of the GSEs' portfolios and guarantees include confidential and proprietary information, it is difficult to reconcile the two different assessments of the GSEs' financial position. In broad terms, the GSEs purchased slightly more than $169 billion of private label subprime MBSs in 2006 and 2007; they purchased slightly less than $58 billion of Alt-A MBSs in the same time period, out of combined total mortgage purchases of $1.677 trillion.[58] At the end of 2007, the subprime and Alt-A MBSs represented 13.5% of the GSEs' total assets.

---

[55] Deborah Solomon, Michael Corkery, and Liz Rappaport, "Mortgage Bailout Is Greeted With Relief, Fresh Questions," *Wall Street Journal*, September 9, 2008, p. A1.

[56] Ibid.

[57] OFHEO, "Statement of OFHEO Director James B. Lockhart," July 10, 2008, available at http://www.fhfa.gov/webfiles/1503/71008Statement.pdf.

[58] OFHEO, *Annual Report to Congress: 2008*, pp. 113 and 116. Subprime and Alt-A MBS purchases prior to 2006 are not available.

Why Did Fannie Mae's and Freddie Mac's Stock Prices Decline in 2008?

Fannie Mae and Freddie Mac are GSEs whose charters limit them to buying single family and multifamily home mortgages originated by others. This lack of diversification makes them more exposed to housing and mortgage market problems than other financial institutions such as commercial banks, which have other lines of business. The GSEs' charters give them a special relationship with the federal government, sometimes called an implicit guarantee, which has allowed them to borrow at interest rates only slightly above those paid by the federal government. In conservatorship, the GSEs have an even closer connection with the government.

The two GSEs were and are very highly leveraged versions of banks: they borrow money to purchase mortgages, and they maximize profits by keeping their capital reserves close to the minimum required by their regulators. Like banks, the GSEs are required by law and by their regulators to maintain a certain ratio between their loans and reserves to protect against loan losses. A key component of reserves is shareholders' equity or the current value of the shareholders' investments. Using funds for capital provides safety, but it is less profitable in normal times than purchasing additional mortgages.

Changes in the perception of the risks that Fannie Mae and Freddie Mac faced—in terms of future profitability and even continued financial viability—reduced the price that investors were willing to pay for a share of the enterprises. There was also concern that intervention by the federal government would reduce the value of the common stock.

Between the end of 2007 and August 1, 2008, Fannie's stock lost 72% of its value, while Freddie's fell by 77%. Between the end of 2007 and September 30, 2008, Fannie Mae's market capitalization fell from $38.8 billion to $825 million, and Freddie Mac's capitalization declined from $26.8 billion to $473 million.[59] As part of Treasury's financial aid package of September 7, 2008, the GSEs agreed to issue warrants to the Treasury worth 79.9% of their outstanding stock. If Treasury were to exercise the warrants, current stockholders would own 20% of each enterprise instead of 100%. This is one explanation why the GSEs' stock prices declined further since September 7, 2008.

What Had Congress Done Previously to Improve the Financial Condition of the GSEs?

Congress had previously assisted GSEs that were in financial difficulty. When Fannie Mae was losing significant amounts of money in 1982, Congress passed the Miscellaneous Revenue Act of 1982 that provided tax benefits for Fannie Mae.[60] The Farm Credit System, another GSE, was aided by the Agricultural Credit Act of 1987, which authorized the issuance of $4 billion in bonds to support system members.[61]

---

[59] Federal Housing Finance Agency, *Report to Congress: 2011*, pp. 121 and 138 available at http://www.fhfa.gov/webfiles/24009/FHFA_RepToCongr11_6_14.pdf.
[60] The Miscellaneous Revenue Act of 1982, P.L. 97-362, 96 Stat. 1726.
[61] The Agricultural Credit Act of 1987, P.L. 100-233, 101 Stat. 1568.

Section 1117 of HERA authorizes the Treasury to purchase any amount of GSE securities—debt or equity—if necessary to provide stability to financial markets, prevent disruptions in the availability of mortgage credit, or protect the taxpayer.[62] This means that if either of the two GSEs became unable to raise funds in private markets, the federal government could purchase the debt securities that the firms were unable to sell elsewhere, or could recapitalize either firm by purchasing stock, possibly becoming the majority shareholder. These contracts sent a signal to the markets that the Treasury was prepared to intervene rather than let either GSE fail.

What Other Actions Has the Federal Government Taken to Address the Financial Condition of the GSEs?

On July 15, 2008, the SEC issued an emergency order restricting short selling in the stock of 19 financial institutions, including Fannie and Freddie.[63] The SEC acted to prevent the possibility that false rumors could drive share prices down and cause the market to lose confidence, thereby cutting off the firms' access to credit markets, as happened to Bear Stearns in March 2008. The order restricting short sales of Fannie Mae and Freddie Mac stock was renewed on July 29, 2008, and expired on August 12, 2008.

The government has also taken steps to prepare for possible future support for the GSEs. On July 13, 2008, the Federal Reserve Board of Governors granted the New York Fed the authority to lend directly to the GSEs.[64] Section 1118 of HERA requires the new GSE regulator to consult with the Fed to ensure financial market stability.

In addition to the Fed's existing general authority to be a lender of last resort, the GSEs' charters give the GSEs a special relationship to the nation's central bank.[65] The Fed can use the GSEs' bonds purchased on the secondary market for open market operations.[66] These bond purchases could indirectly help the GSEs by adding to the demand for their debt and increasing their liquidity. The Fed announced that it would conduct a special program to purchase GSE debt and MBSs in calendar 2009 and the first quarter of 2010.[67] Under this program, the Fed purchased more than $1 trillion of GSE debt and GSE-issued MBSs.

In programs that started in September 2008 and ended in March 2010, the Fed and Treasury together purchased $1,135.9 billion in MBSs.[68] On September 21, 2011, the Fed decided to begin

---

[62] The Housing and Economic Recovery Act of 2008, P.L. 110-289, Sec. 117.

[63] Securities and Exchange Commission, "Emergency Order Pursuant to Section 12(k)(2) of the Securities Exchange Act of 1934 Taking Temporary Action to Respond to Market Developments," available at http://www.sec.gov/rules/other/2008/34-58166.pdf.

[64] Federal Reserve Board of Governors, "Authority to Lend to Fannie Mae and Freddie Mac," press release, July 13, 2008, available at http://www.federalreserve.gov/newsevents/press/other/20080713a.htm.

[65] The Fed's lender-of-last-resort authority is delineated at 12 U.S.C. 343. Fannie Mae's charter is at 12 U.S.C. 1716b et seq., and Freddie Mac's charter is at 12 U.S.C. 1401.

[66] 12 U.S.C. 347c.

[67] Federal Reserve Bank of New York, "FAQs: MBS Purchase Program," August 20, 2010, available at http://www.ny.frb.org/markets/mbs_faq.html.

[68] Federal Housing Finance Agency, "Data as of June 10, 2012, on Treasury and Federal Reserve Purchase Programs for GSE and Mortgage-Related Securities," available at http://www.fhfa.gov/webfiles/24022/TSYSupport%202012-06-20.pdf.

reinvesting MBS principal repayments in other MBSs.[69] As of the end of the second quarter of 2012, the Fed held $855.0 billion of Fannie Mae's and Freddie Mac's MBSs.[70]

Who Has Invested in the Fannie Mae and Freddie Mac?

There is little information available about who holds GSE stock, bonds, and MBSs. The Fed reports statistics for combined ownership of government agency and GSE debt and GSE MBSs. At the first quarter of 2012, non-U.S. investors held $999 billion of $7.5 trillion agency and GSE securities.[71] Other large investors were U.S.-chartered depository institutions ($1.7 trillion), life insurance companies ($387 billion), state and local government retirement funds ($290 billion), mutual funds ($1.0 trillion), and the GSEs themselves ($348 billion).

Fannie Mae reports that central bank ownership of certain types of debt declined from 41.1% at the end of 2008 to 15.6% as of May 21, 2012.[72] Freddie Mac showed central bank ownership of its debt declined from slightly less than 40% of the outstanding debt at the end of 2008 to 28% as of May 31, 2012.[73]

What Recent Legislation Has Affected the GSEs?

Since the 110th Congress, five bills and two continuing resolutions have been signed into law that have had significant impacts on Fannie Mae, and Freddie Mac. (See **Table 5**.)

In the 112th Congress, several bills, which have not become law, have been introduced to reform the GSEs. See CRS Report R41822, *Proposals to Reform Fannie Mae and Freddie Mac in the 112th Congress*, by N. Eric Weiss for information on these proposals. In addition, other legislation, discussed in CRS Report RS22172, *The Conforming Loan Limit*, by N. Eric Weiss and Sean M. Hoskins, has been introduced to permit the GSEs to purchase larger mortgages.

---

[69] Federal Reserve Bank of New York, "FAQs: Reinvestments of Principal Payments on Agency Securities into Agency MBS," September 26, 2011, available at http://www.newyorkfed.org/markets/ambs/ambs_faq.html.

[70] Federal Reserve Bank of New York, "System Open Market Account Holdings: Securities Holdings as of June 27, 2012," available at http://www.newyorkfed.org/markets/soma/sysopen_accholdings.html.

[71] Federal Reserve, "Agency- and GSE-backed Securities," *Flow of Funds Accounts of the United States*, June 7, 2012, Table L. 210, available at http://www.federalreserve.gov/releases/z1/.

[72] Fannie Mae, "Noncallable Benchmark Notes Distribution Reports," *Benchmark Securities*, YTD 2012, available at http://www.fanniemae.com/resources/file/debt/pdf/benchmark-securities/2012_benchmark_distribution.pdf.

[73] Freddie Mac, *Freddie Mac Update*, June 2012, available at http://www.freddiemac.com/investors/pdffiles/investor-presentation.pdf.

Table 5. Public Laws Specifically Affecting GSEs
(passed in 110th, 111th, and 112th Congresses)

P.L. Number	Date Enacted	Title	Summary
P.L. 110-185	February 13, 2008	Economic Stimulus Act of 2008 (ESA)	Increased conforming loan limits in high-cost areas for mortgages originated between July 1, 2007 and December 31, 2008.
P.L. 110-289	July 30, 2008	Housing and Economic Recovery Act of 2008 (HERA)	Created Federal Housing Finance Agency to replace Office of Federal Housing Enterprise Oversight and the Department of Housing and Urban Development as combined GSE regulator. Made high-cost area conforming loan limits permanent, but at lower amounts.
P.L. 111-5	February 7, 2009	American Recovery and Reinvestment Act of 2009 (ARRA)	Extended 2008 high-cost conforming loan limits to 2009 mortgages.
P.L. 111-88	October 30, 2009	Department of Interior Appropriations Act for FY2010	Extended 2008 high-cost conforming loan limits for FY2010.
P.L. 111-242	September 30, 2010	Continuing Appropriations Act of 2011	Extended 2008 high-cost conforming loan limits for FY2011.
P.L. 112-78	December 23, 2011	Temporary Payroll Tax Cut Continuation Act of 2011	Requires Fannie Mae and Freddie Mac to increase their guarantee fees by 10 basis points. The funds raised are to be deposited in the Treasury.
P.L. 112-105	April 4, 2012	Stop Trading on Congressional Knowledge Act of 2012	Prohibition on bonuses to executives of Fannie Mae and Freddie Mac while they are in conservatorship.

Source: Congressional Research Service.

Glossary

Agency bonds	In this report, agency bonds are those issued by Fannie Mae, Freddie Mac, and Ginnie Mae. Fannie Mae and Freddie Mac are stockholder-owned government-sponsored enterprises. Ginnie Mae is part of the Department of Housing and Urban Development.
Alt-A mortgage	Either a mortgage made to a borrower with a credit history between prime and subprime, or a mortgage made to a prime borrower with less than traditional documentation.
ARRA	American Recovery and Reinvestment Act of 2009, P.L. 111-5, 123 Stat. 115.
ESA	Economic Stimulus Act of 2008, P.L. 110-185, 122 Stat. 613,
FHFA	Federal Housing Finance Agency. Regulator of housing GSEs for mission, safety and soundness. Created by merger of existing government agencies, including OFHEO and HUD staff (who formerly had mission regulatory authority).
GSE	Government-sponsored enterprise.
GSECF	Government-sponsored enterprise credit facility. The Treasury's program to lend money to Fannie Mae, Freddie Mac, and the Federal Home Loan Banks using MBSs as collateral. This program expired December 31, 2009, and had been authorized by HERA.
HERA	Housing and Economic Recovery Act of 2008, P.L. 110-289, 122 Stat. 2654.
MBSs	Mortgage-backed securities. A pool of mortgages sold to institutional investors.
OFHEO	Office of Federal Housing Enterprise. Safety and soundness regulator for Fannie Mae and Freddie Mac. Merged into Federal Housing Finance Agency.
Prime mortgage	A mortgage made to a borrower with excellent credit history.
Private-label MBSs	Mortgage-backed securities underwritten and sold by commercial and investment banks. They are not created by the GSEs or a government agency.
Senior preferred stock	This stock is senior to (has priority over) all other common and preferred stock; it is the only GSE stock currently receiving dividends.
Subprime mortgage	A mortgage made to a borrower with a blemished credit history.

Author Contact Information

N. Eric Weiss
Specialist in Financial Economics
eweiss@crs.loc.gov, 7-6209

www.ingramcontent.com/pod-product-compliance
Lightning Source LLC
Chambersburg PA
CBHW081246180526
45171CB00005B/565